AROUND THE CAMPFIRE

HUNTING AND FISHING JOURNAL
TO RECORD YOUR MEMORIES AND TROPHIES

The quoted ideas expressed in this book (but not scripture verses) are not, in all cases, exact quotations, as some have been edited for clarity and brevity. In all cases, the author has attempted to maintain the speaker's original intent. In some cases, quoted material for this book was obtained from secondary sources, primarily print media. While every effort was made to ensure the accuracy of these sources, the accuracy cannot be guaranteed.

For additions, deletions, corrections, or clarifications in future editions of this text, please contact Paul Shepherd, Executive Director for Elm Hill Books.
Email pshepherd@elmhillbooks.com.

Scripture quotations are taken from:

The Holy Bible, New King James Version (NKJV) Copyright © 1982 by Thomas Nelson, Inc. Used by permission.

Cover Design by Karen Phillips
Page Layout by Bart Dawson

ISBN 1-4041-8511-9

Printed in the United States of America

Finally. A book to write of your trophies and a place to record your stories about those great hunts and catches you can share with friends; stored for "looking back" in years to come. We've heard from hunters and fisherman that you keep pictures as you enjoy each season. And we've heard you wish you could keep a history of all your memorable moments in one place. Hopefully, our journal will give you that place…a place to put photos, write about your adventures and remember key locations before starting again next year. May all your shots be perfect, and your lures do their stuff.

The Publisher

HUNTING JOURNAL

Typical Game:

Alaska Brown Bear
Black Bear
Grizzly Bear
Polar Bear
Bison
Barren Ground Caribou
Mountain Caribou
Quebec-Labrador Caribou
Woodland Caribou
Cougar
Columbian Blacktail Deer
Sitka Blacktail Deer
Coues' Deer
Mule Deer

Whitetail Deer
Roosevelt's / Olympic Elk
Yellowstone / Wapiti Elk
Rocky Mountain Goat
Alaska-Yukon Moose
Canada Moose
Shiras Moose
Muskox
Pronghorn Antelope
Bighorn Sheep
Dall's Sheep
Desert Bighorn Sheep
Stone's Sheep

GAME HUNTED: _Whitetail Deer_

> "He makes my feet like the feet of the deer,
> and set me on high places."
> *Psalm 18:33*

Date _November 12, 2004_

Location _Adirondacks, NY_

Weather _Overcast and Cool_

Hunting Partner _John Smith_

Type of Hunt | Gun ☒ | Bow |
| Muzzle Loader |

NOTES

Thoughts and Comments of the Day

_John and I set off about 5 am. We went off
to the west to our usual lucky spot. After a
two hour wait I spotted a real good one, took
aim and shot. I got a good clean kill. After
we got it back to camp the rest of the boys
showed up just in time to celebrate._

GAME HARVESTED

Time _7:35_   Gun Used _Winchester 70_

Bullet Weight _.30/06_   Number of Pulls _1_

Powder _____   Arrows _____

Number of Points _10_   B&C Rating _141_

[inside] _17-5_   [   ]_____

[outside] _19-5_   [   ]_____

———— PRIZE PHOTO ————

Insert Photo of Whitetail Deer

GAME HUNTED: _____

> *...for it is God who works in you both to will*
> *and to do for His good pleasure.*
> *Philippians 2:13*

Date _____

Location _____

Weather _____

Hunting Partner _____

Type of Hunt | Gun | | Bow |
Muzzle Loader

NOTES

Thoughts and Comments of the Day

_____

_____

_____

_____

_____

_____

_____

_____

_____

GAME HARVESTED

Time _____   Gun Used _____

Bullet Weight _____   Number of Pulls _____

Powder _____   Arrows _____

Number of Points _____   B&C Rating _____

[   ]_____   [   ]_____

[   ]_____   [   ]_____

——— PRIZE PHOTO ———

GAME HUNTED: _____

> *I can do all things through Christ who strengthens me.*
> *Philippians 4:13*

Date _____

Location _____

Weather _____

Hunting Partner _____

Type of Hunt | Gun | Bow |
| Muzzle Loader |

NOTES

Thoughts and Comments of the Day

_____
_____
_____
_____
_____
_____
_____
_____
_____

GAME HARVESTED

Time _____   Gun Used _____

Bullet Weight _____   Number of Pulls _____

Powder _____   Arrows _____

Number of Points _____   B&C Rating _____

[   ] _____   [   ] _____

[   ] _____   [   ] _____

———— PRIZE PHOTO ————

GAME HUNTED: _____

Standing like an enemy, He has bent His bow;
With His right hand, like an adversary.
Lamentations 2:4

Date _____

Location _____

Weather _____

Hunting Partner _____

Type of Hunt Gun   Bow
              Muzzle Loader

NOTES

Thoughts and Comments of the Day

_____
_____
_____
_____
_____
_____
_____
_____
_____
_____

GAME HARVESTED

Time _____ Gun Used _____

Bullet Weight _____ Number of Pulls _____

Powder _____ Arrows _____

Number of Points _____ B&C Rating _____

[   ]_____ [   ]_____

[   ]_____ [   ]_____

———— PRIZE PHOTO ————

GAME HUNTED: _____

> *Their wings touched one another. The creatures did not turn when they went, but each one went straight forward.*
> *Ezekiel 1:9*

Date _____

Location _____

Weather _____

Hunting Partner _____

Type of Hunt | Gun | | Bow |
| Muzzle Loader |

NOTES

Thoughts and Comments of the Day

_____

_____

_____

_____

_____

_____

_____

_____

_____

GAME HARVESTED

Time _____   Gun Used _____

Bullet Weight _____   Number of Pulls _____

Powder _____   Arrows _____

Number of Points _____   B&C Rating _____

[   ]_____   [   ]_____

[   ]_____   [   ]_____

——— PRIZE PHOTO ———

GAME HUNTED: _____

> *He was a mighty hunter before the Lord...*
> *Genesis 10:9*

Date _____

Location _____

Weather _____

Hunting Partner _____

Type of Hunt [Gun] [Bow]
[Muzzle Loader]

NOTES

Thoughts and Comments of the Day

_____

_____

_____

_____

_____

_____

_____

_____

_____

GAME HARVESTED

Time _____   Gun Used _____

Bullet Weight _____   Number of Pulls _____

Powder _____   Arrows _____

Number of Points _____   B&C Rating _____

[   ]_____   [   ]_____

[   ]_____   [   ]_____

———— PRIZE PHOTO ————

GAME HUNTED: _____

> "And He has made My mouth like a sharp sword;
> In the shadow of His hand He has hidden Me, And made Me
> a polished shaft; In His quiver He has hidden Me."
> *Isaiah 49:2*

Date _____

Location _____

Weather _____

Hunting Partner _____

Type of Hunt | Gun | | Bow |
| Muzzle Loader |

NOTES

Thoughts and Comments of the Day

_____

_____

_____

_____

_____

_____

_____

_____

_____

GAME HARVESTED

Time _____   Gun Used _____

Bullet Weight _____   Number of Pulls _____

Powder _____   Arrows _____

Number of Points _____   B&C Rating _____

[   ]_____   [   ]_____

[   ]_____   [   ]_____

———— PRIZE PHOTO ————

GAME HUNTED: _____

> *...so that they should seek the Lord, in the hope that*
> *they might grope for Him and find Him,*
> *though He is not far from each one of us.*
> Acts 17:27

Date _____

Location _____

Weather _____

Hunting Partner _____

Type of Hunt | Gun | | Bow |
| Muzzle Loader |

NOTES

Thoughts and Comments of the Day

_____

_____

_____

_____

_____

_____

_____

_____

_____

_____

GAME HARVESTED

Time _____   Gun Used _____

Bullet Weight _____   Number of Pulls _____

Powder _____   Arrows _____

Number of Points _____   B&C Rating _____

[   ]_____   [   ]_____

[   ]_____   [   ]_____

—————— PRIZE PHOTO ——————

GAME HUNTED: _____

> *Come and see the works of God;*
> *He is awesome in His doing toward the sons of men.*
> *Psalms 66:5*

Date _____

Location _____

Weather _____

Hunting Partner _____

Type of Hunt   Gun   Bow
               Muzzle Loader

NOTES

Thoughts and Comments of the Day

_____

_____

_____

_____

_____

_____

_____

_____

_____

_____

GAME HARVESTED

Time _____   Gun Used _____

Bullet Weight _____   Number of Pulls _____

Powder _____   Arrows _____

Number of Points _____   B&C Rating _____

[   ] _____   [   ] _____

[   ] _____   [   ] _____

——— PRIZE PHOTO ———

GAME HUNTED: _____

> *Fathers, do not provoke your children,*
> *lest they become discouraged.*
> Colossians 3:21

Date _____

Location _____

Weather _____

Hunting Partner _____

Type of Hunt | Gun | | Bow |

| Muzzle Loader |

Thoughts and Comments of the Day

_____

_____

_____

_____

_____

_____

_____

_____

NOTES

GAME HARVESTED

Time _____   Gun Used _____

Bullet Weight _____   Number of Pulls _____

Powder _____   Arrows _____

Number of Points _____   B&C Rating _____

[   ]_____   [   ]_____

[   ]_____   [   ]_____

———— PRIZE PHOTO ————

GAME HUNTED: _____

> *Happy is the man who has his quiver full of them;*
> *They shall not be ashamed,*
> *But shall speak with their enemies in the gate.*
> *Psalms 127:5*

Date _____

Location _____

Weather _____

Hunting Partner _____

Type of Hunt ☐ Gun   ☐ Bow
☐ Muzzle Loader

Thoughts and Comments of the Day

_____

_____

_____

_____

_____

_____

_____

_____

_____

NOTES

GAME HARVESTED

Time _____   Gun Used _____

Bullet Weight _____   Number of Pulls _____

Powder _____   Arrows _____

Number of Points _____   B&C Rating _____

[   ] _____   [   ] _____

[   ] _____   [   ] _____

———— PRIZE PHOTO ————

GAME HUNTED: _____

> *When I heard, my body trembled; My lips quivered at the voice;*
> *Rottenness entered my bones; And I trembled in myself.*
> *Habakkuk 3:16*

Date _____

Location _____

Weather _____

Hunting Partner _____

Type of Hunt Gun   Bow

Muzzle Loader

Thoughts and Comments of the Day

_____

_____

_____

_____

_____

_____

_____

_____

_____

NOTES

GAME HARVESTED

Time _____   Gun Used _____

Bullet Weight _____   Number of Pulls _____

Powder _____   Arrows _____

Number of Points _____   B&C Rating _____

[   ]_____   [   ]_____

[   ]_____   [   ]_____

——— PRIZE PHOTO ———

GAME HUNTED: _____

> *He also had made savory food, and brought it to his father,*
> *and said to his father, "Let my father arise and eat*
> *of his son's game, that your soul may bless me."*
> Genesis 27:31

Date _____

Location _____

Weather _____

Hunting Partner _____

Type of Hunt | Gun | | Bow |
 | Muzzle Loader |

NOTES

Thoughts and Comments of the Day

_____

_____

_____

_____

_____

_____

_____

_____

_____

GAME HARVESTED

Time _____   Gun Used _____

Bullet Weight _____   Number of Pulls _____

Powder _____   Arrows _____

Number of Points _____   B&C Rating _____

[   ]_____   [   ]_____

[   ]_____   [   ]_____

———— PRIZE PHOTO ————

GAME HUNTED: _____

> *Like arrows in the hand of a warrior,*
> *So are the children of one's youth.*
> *Psalms 127:4*

Date _____

Location _____

Weather _____

Hunting Partner _____

Type of Hunt [Gun] [Bow]
[Muzzle Loader]

NOTES

Thoughts and Comments of the Day

_____
_____
_____
_____
_____
_____
_____
_____
_____
_____

GAME HARVESTED

Time _____   Gun Used _____

Bullet Weight _____   Number of Pulls _____

Powder _____   Arrows _____

Number of Points _____   B&C Rating _____

[   ]_____   [   ]_____

[   ]_____   [   ]_____

——— PRIZE PHOTO ———

GAME HUNTED: _____

> ...holding fast the word of life, so that I may rejoice in
> the day of Christ that I have not run in vain or labored in vain.
> *Philippians 2:16*

Date _____

Location _____

Weather _____

Hunting Partner _____

Type of Hunt Gun   Bow
              Muzzle Loader

NOTES

Thoughts and Comments of the Day

_____

_____

_____

_____

_____

_____

_____

_____

_____

_____

GAME HARVESTED

Time _____ Gun Used _____

Bullet Weight _____ Number of Pulls _____

Powder _____ Arrows _____

Number of Points _____ B&C Rating _____

[   ] _____ [   ] _____

[   ] _____ [   ] _____

——— PRIZE PHOTO ———

GAME HUNTED: _____

> *Now therefore, please take your weapons, your quiver*
> *and your bow, and go out to the field and hunt game for me.*
> *Genesis 27:3*

Date _____

Location _____

Weather _____

Hunting Partner _____

Type of Hunt | Gun | | Bow |

| Muzzle Loader |

| NOTES |

Thoughts and Comments of the Day

_____

_____

_____

_____

_____

_____

_____

_____

_____

GAME HARVESTED

Time _____   Gun Used _____

Bullet Weight _____   Number of Pulls _____

Powder _____   Arrows _____

Number of Points _____   B&C Rating _____

[   ]_____   [   ]_____

[   ]_____   [   ]_____

——— PRIZE PHOTO ———

GAME HUNTED: _____

> And when they had prayed, the place where they were
> assembled together was shaken; and they were all filled with
> the Holy Spirit, and they spoke the word of God with boldness.
> *Acts 4:31*

Date _____

Location _____

Weather _____

Hunting Partner _____

Type of Hunt [Gun]   [Bow]
             [Muzzle Loader]

NOTES

Thoughts and Comments of the Day

_____
_____
_____
_____
_____
_____
_____
_____
_____

GAME HARVESTED

Time _____   Gun Used _____

Bullet Weight _____   Number of Pulls _____

Powder _____   Arrows _____

Number of Points _____   B&C Rating _____

[   ]_____   [   ]_____

[   ]_____   [   ]_____

——— PRIZE PHOTO ———

GAME HUNTED: _____

> *Now Rebekah was listening when Isaac spoke to Esau his son.*
> *And Esau went to the field to hunt game and to bring it.*
> *Genesis 27:5*

Date _____

Location _____

Weather _____

Hunting Partner _____

Type of Hunt | Gun | | Bow |
 | Muzzle Loader |

NOTES

Thoughts and Comments of the Day

_____
_____
_____
_____
_____
_____
_____
_____
_____
_____

GAME HARVESTED

Time _____   Gun Used _____

Bullet Weight _____   Number of Pulls _____

Powder _____   Arrows _____

Number of Points _____   B&C Rating _____

[   ] _____   [   ] _____

[   ] _____   [   ] _____

———— PRIZE PHOTO ————

GAME HUNTED: _____

> *And the people stayed up all that day, all night,
> and all the next day, and gathered the quail
> (he who gathered least gathered ten homers); and they
> spread them out for themselves all around the camp.*
> Numbers 11:32

Date _____

Location _____

Weather _____

Hunting Partner _____

Type of Hunt | Gun | | Bow |
| Muzzle Loader |

NOTES

Thoughts and Comments of the Day

_____

_____

_____

_____

_____

_____

_____

_____

_____

GAME HARVESTED

Time _____   Gun Used _____

Bullet Weight _____   Number of Pulls _____

Powder _____   Arrows _____

Number of Points _____   B&C Rating _____

[   ]_____   [   ]_____

[   ]_____   [   ]_____

———— PRIZE PHOTO ————

GAME HUNTED: _____

So that men will say, "Surely there is a reward for the righteous;
Surely He is God who judges in the earth."
Psalms 58:11

Date _____

Location _____

Weather _____

Hunting Partner _____

Type of Hunt Gun ☐   Bow ☐
              Muzzle Loader ☐

Thoughts and Comments of the Day

_____

_____

_____

_____

_____

_____

_____

_____

_____

_____

NOTES

GAME HARVESTED

Time _____   Gun Used _____

Bullet Weight _____   Number of Pulls _____

Powder _____   Arrows _____

Number of Points _____   B&C Rating _____

[   ]_____   [   ]_____

[   ]_____   [   ]_____

———— PRIZE PHOTO ————

GAME HUNTED: _____

> *In all your ways acknowledge Him,*
> *And He shall direct your paths.*
> Proverbs 3:6

Date _____

Location _____

Weather _____

Hunting Partner _____

Type of Hunt | Gun | | Bow |

| Muzzle Loader |

Thoughts and Comments of the Day

_____

_____

_____

_____

_____

_____

_____

_____

NOTES

GAME HARVESTED

Time _____ Gun Used _____

Bullet Weight _____ Number of Pulls _____

Powder _____ Arrows _____

Number of Points _____ B&C Rating _____

[   ] _____ [   ] _____

[   ] _____ [   ] _____

———— PRIZE PHOTO ————

GAME HUNTED: _____

So the boys grew. And Esau was a skillful hunter,
a man of the field; but Jacob was a mild man, dwelling in tents.
Genesis 25:27

Date _____

Location _____

Weather _____

Hunting Partner _____

Type of Hunt | Gun | Bow |
| Muzzle Loader |

NOTES

Thoughts and Comments of the Day

_____
_____
_____
_____
_____
_____
_____
_____
_____

GAME HARVESTED

Time _____   Gun Used _____

Bullet Weight _____   Number of Pulls _____

Powder _____   Arrows _____

Number of Points _____   B&C Rating _____

[   ]_____   [   ]_____

[   ]_____   [   ]_____

———— PRIZE PHOTO ————

GAME HUNTED: _____

> *Hear attentively the thunder of His voice,*
> *And the rumbling that comes from His mouth.*
> *Job 37:2*

Date _____

Location _____

Weather _____

Hunting Partner _____

Type of Hunt | Gun | | Bow |
              | Muzzle Loader |

NOTES

Thoughts and Comments of the Day

_____

_____

_____

_____

_____

_____

_____

_____

_____

Game Harvested

Time _____ Gun Used _____

Bullet Weight _____ Number of Pulls _____

Powder _____ Arrows _____

Number of Points _____ B&C Rating _____

[   ]_____ [   ]_____

[   ]_____ [   ]_____

——— PRIZE PHOTO ———

GAME HUNTED: _____

> *Then God blessed them, and God said to them,*
> *"Be fruitful and multiply; fill the earth and subdue it;*
> *have dominion over the fish of the sea, over the birds of the air,*
> *and over every living thing that moves on the earth."*
> Genesis 1:28

Date _____

Location _____

Weather _____

Hunting Partner _____

Type of Hunt [Gun]   [Bow]
[Muzzle Loader]

Thoughts and Comments of the Day

_____

_____

_____

_____

_____

_____

_____

_____

_____

_____

NOTES

Game Harvested

Time _____   Gun Used _____

Bullet Weight _____   Number of Pulls _____

Powder _____   Arrows _____

Number of Points _____   B&C Rating _____

[   ]_____   [   ]_____

[   ]_____   [   ]_____

———— PRIZE PHOTO ————

GAME HUNTED: _____

> *The lazy man does not roast what he took in hunting,*
> *But diligence is man's precious possession.*
> *Proverbs 12:27*

Date _____

Location _____

Weather _____

Hunting Partner _____

Type of Hunt | Gun | Bow |
| Muzzle Loader |

NOTES

Thoughts and Comments of the Day

_____

_____

_____

_____

_____

_____

_____

_____

_____

GAME HARVESTED

Time _____   Gun Used _____

Bullet Weight _____   Number of Pulls _____

Powder _____   Arrows _____

Number of Points _____   B&C Rating _____

[   ]_____   [   ]_____

[   ]_____   [   ]_____

——— PRIZE PHOTO ———

GAME HUNTED: _____

> *He makes my feet like the feet of deer,*
> *And sets me on my high places.*
> *Psalms 18:33*

Date _____

Location _____

Weather _____

Hunting Partner _____

Type of Hunt | Gun | | Bow |
| Muzzle Loader |

Thoughts and Comments of the Day

NOTES

_____

_____

_____

_____

_____

_____

_____

_____

_____

_____

GAME HARVESTED

Time _____   Gun Used _____

Bullet Weight _____   Number of Pulls _____

Powder _____   Arrows _____

Number of Points _____   B&C Rating _____

[   ] _____   [   ] _____

[   ] _____   [   ] _____

——— PRIZE PHOTO ———

GAME HUNTED: _____

> *For among My people are found wicked men;*
> *They lie in wait as one who sets snares;*
> *They set a trap; They catch men.*
> *Jeremiah 5:26*

Date _____

Location _____

Weather _____

Hunting Partner _____

Type of Hunt | Gun | | Bow |
| Muzzle Loader |

NOTES

Thoughts and Comments of the Day

_____
_____
_____
_____
_____
_____
_____
_____
_____
_____

GAME HARVESTED

Time _____   Gun Used _____

Bullet Weight _____   Number of Pulls _____

Powder _____   Arrows _____

Number of Points _____   B&C Rating _____

[   ]_____   [   ]_____

[   ]_____   [   ]_____

———— PRIZE PHOTO ————

GAME HUNTED: _____

> *So God was with the lad; and he grew and dwelt*
> *in the wilderness, and became an archer.*
> *Genesis 21:20*

Date _____

Location _____

Weather _____

Hunting Partner _____

Type of Hunt | Gun | | Bow |
| Muzzle Loader |

NOTES

Thoughts and Comments of the Day

_____

_____

_____

_____

_____

_____

_____

_____

_____

GAME HARVESTED

Time _____   Gun Used _____

Bullet Weight _____   Number of Pulls _____

Powder _____   Arrows _____

Number of Points _____   B&C Rating _____

[   ]_____   [   ]_____

[   ]_____   [   ]_____

——— PRIZE PHOTO ———

GAME HUNTED: _____

The voice of one crying in the wilderness:
"Prepare the way of the Lord; Make straight in the desert
A highway for our God."
Isaiah 40:3

Date _____

Location _____

Weather _____

Hunting Partner _____

Type of Hunt [Gun] [Bow]
[Muzzle Loader]

Thoughts and Comments of the Day

_____

_____

_____

_____

_____

_____

_____

_____

_____

NOTES

GAME HARVESTED

Time _____   Gun Used _____

Bullet Weight _____   Number of Pulls _____

Powder _____   Arrows _____

Number of Points _____   B&C Rating _____

[   ]_____   [   ]_____

[   ]_____   [   ]_____

———— PRIZE PHOTO ————

GAME HUNTED: _____

> *For I will not trust in my bow,*
> *Nor shall my sword save me.*
> *Psalms 44:6*

Date _____

Location _____

Weather _____

Hunting Partner _____

Type of Hunt | Gun | | Bow |

| Muzzle Loader |

NOTES

Thoughts and Comments of the Day

_____

_____

_____

_____

_____

_____

_____

_____

_____

_____

GAME HARVESTED

Time _____   Gun Used _____

Bullet Weight _____   Number of Pulls _____

Powder _____   Arrows _____

Number of Points _____   B&C Rating _____

[   ]_____   [   ]_____

[   ]_____   [   ]_____

———— PRIZE PHOTO ————

GAME HUNTED: _____

> *But his bow remained in strength, And the arms of his hands were made strong By the hands of the Mighty God of Jacob (From there is the Shepherd, the Stone of Israel).*
> Genesis 49:24

Date _____

Location _____

Weather _____

Hunting Partner _____

Type of Hunt | Gun | | Bow |
| Muzzle Loader |

NOTES

Thoughts and Comments of the Day

_____
_____
_____
_____
_____
_____
_____
_____
_____

GAME HARVESTED

Time _____   Gun Used _____

Bullet Weight _____   Number of Pulls _____

Powder _____   Arrows _____

Number of Points _____   B&C Rating _____

[   ]_____   [   ]_____

[   ]_____   [   ]_____

———— PRIZE PHOTO ————

BIRD HUNTING JOURNAL

Typical Bird Game:

Coot
Mourning Dove
White-winged Dove
Mallard Duck
Pintail Duck
Wood Duck
Canvasback Duck
Gallinules
Blue Geese
Cananda Geese
Snow Geese
Ross' Geese
Ruffled Grouse
Spruce Grouse
Sage Grouse

Chukar Partridge
Hungarian Partridge
Pheasant
Ptarmigan
Bobtail Quail
Califorinia Quail
Gambel's Quail
Mearn's Quail
Scaled Quail
Virginia Rail
Sora Rail
Snipe
Wild Turkey
Woodcock

BIRD HUNTED: __Ruffled Grouse__

> *And you will seek Me and find Me,*
> *when you search for Me with all your heart.*
> Jeremiah 29:13

Date __September 12, 2004__

Location __Idaho__

Weather __Clear and Cool__

Hunting Partners __John Smith__

__Bill Walker, Walt Farmer__

NOTES

Camouflage

Map

Thoughts and Comments of the Day

We all set off about 7 am from camp. We went up north today. Rode for half an hour on 4-wheelers. We let the dogs loose, Walt and I followed Jo Jo. She ran straight for a gathering of trees and drove several birds out. Walt got one ruffled. The next spot Jo Jo found was my time to shine. I got two good sized ruffled. After we got back to camp for lunch our guide took our group photo.

BIRDS HARVESTED

Time _about 8:30am_   Gun Used _Remmington 870_

Bullet Weight _____   Number of Pulls _____3_____

Days at Camp __2_____   Dogs _Eng. Setter - Jo Jo___

Guide __Mark Cooper_____   Equipment Used _____

[# of Birds] _2_____   [   ]_____

[   ]_____   [   ]_____

———— PRIZE PHOTO ————

Insert Photo of
Ruffled Grouse

BIRD HUNTED: _____

> *Put on the whole armor of God,*
> *that you may be able to stand against the wiles of the devil.*
> *Ephesians 6:11*

Date _____

Location _____

Weather _____

Hunting Partners _____

_____

NOTES

Thoughts and Comments of the Day

_____
_____
_____
_____
_____
_____
_____
_____
_____
_____

BIRDS HARVESTED

Time _____   Gun Used _____

Bullet Weight _____   Number of Pulls _____

Days at Camp _____   Dogs _____

Guide _____   Equipment Used _____

[   ]_____   [   ]_____

[   ]_____   [   ]_____

———— PRIZE PHOTO ————

BIRD HUNTED: _____

The young lions lack and suffer hunger;
But those who seek the Lord shall not lack any good thing.
Psalms 34:10

Date _____

Location _____

Weather _____

Hunting Partners _____

_____

NOTES

Thoughts and Comments of the Day

_____
_____
_____
_____
_____
_____
_____
_____
_____

BIRDS HARVESTED

Time _____   Gun Used _____

Bullet Weight _____   Number of Pulls _____

Days at Camp _____   Dogs _____

Guide _____   Equipment Used _____

[   ]_____   [   ]_____

[   ]_____   [   ]_____

———— PRIZE PHOTO ————

BIRD HUNTED: _____

> *Be diligent to present yourself approved to God,*
> *a worker who does not need to be ashamed,*
> *rightly dividing the word of truth.* .
> 2 Timothy 2:15

Date _____

Location _____

Weather _____

Hunting Partners _____

_____

NOTES

Thoughts and Comments of the Day

_____

_____

_____

_____

_____

_____

_____

_____

BIRDS HARVESTED

Time _____   Gun Used _____

Bullet Weight _____   Number of Pulls _____

Days at Camp _____   Dogs _____

Guide _____   Equipment Used _____

[   ] _____   [   ] _____

[   ] _____   [   ] _____

———— PRIZE PHOTO ————

BIRD HUNTED: _____

> *I am the good shepherd; and I know My sheep,*
> *and am known by My own.*
> John 10:14

Date _____

Location _____

Weather _____

Hunting Partners _____

_____

NOTES

Thoughts and Comments of the Day

_____

_____

_____

_____

_____

_____

_____

_____

_____

_____

BIRDS HARVESTED

Time _____   Gun Used _____

Bullet Weight _____   Number of Pulls _____

Days at Camp _____   Dogs _____

Guide _____   Equipment Used _____

[   ]_____   [   ]_____

[   ]_____   [   ]_____

———— PRIZE PHOTO ————

BIRD HUNTED: _____

Trust in the Lord with all your heart,
And lean not on your own understanding;
Proverbs 3:5

Date _____

Location _____

Weather _____

Hunting Partners _____

_____

NOTES

Thoughts and Comments of the Day

_____

_____

_____

_____

_____

_____

_____

_____

_____

BIRDS HARVESTED

Time _____   Gun Used _____

Bullet Weight _____   Number of Pulls _____

Days at Camp _____   Dogs _____

Guide _____   Equipment Used _____

[   ]_____   [   ]_____

[   ]_____   [   ]_____

———— PRIZE PHOTO ————

BIRD HUNTED: _____

> *Blessed is the man who endures temptation; for when*
> *he has been approved, he will receive the crown of life*
> *which the Lord has promised to those who love Him.*
> *James 1:12*

Date _____

Location _____

Weather _____

Hunting Partners _____

_____

NOTES

Thoughts and Comments of the Day

_____
_____
_____
_____
_____
_____
_____
_____
_____

BIRDS HARVESTED

Time _____   Gun Used _____

Bullet Weight _____   Number of Pulls _____

Days at Camp _____   Dogs _____

Guide _____   Equipment Used _____

[   ]_____   [   ]_____

[   ]_____   [   ]_____

——— PRIZE PHOTO ———

BIRD HUNTED: _____

> *If my head is exalted, You hunt me like a fierce lion,*
> *And again You show Yourself awesome against me.*
> *Job 10:16*

Date _____

Location _____

Weather _____

Hunting Partners _____

_____

NOTES

Thoughts and Comments of the Day

_____

_____

_____

_____

_____

_____

_____

_____

Birds Harvested

Time _____   Gun Used _____

Bullet Weight _____   Number of Pulls _____

Days at Camp _____   Dogs _____

Guide _____   Equipment Used _____

[   ]_____   [   ]_____

[   ]_____   [   ]_____

———— PRIZE PHOTO ————

BIRD HUNTED: _____

Prepare your outside work, Make it fit for yourself in the field;
And afterward build your house.
Proverbs 24:27

Date _____

Location _____

Weather _____

Hunting Partners _____

_____

NOTES

Thoughts and Comments of the Day

_____
_____
_____
_____
_____
_____
_____
_____
_____
_____

BIRDS HARVESTED

Time _____   Gun Used _____

Bullet Weight _____   Number of Pulls _____

Days at Camp _____   Dogs _____

Guide _____   Equipment Used _____

[   ]_____   [   ]_____

[   ]_____   [   ]_____

———— PRIZE PHOTO ————

BIRD HUNTED: _____

> *Oh, that you had heeded My commandments!*
> *Then your peace would have been like a river...*
> Isaiah 48:18

Date _____

Location _____

Weather _____

Hunting Partners _____

_____

NOTES

Thoughts and Comments of the Day

_____

_____

_____

_____

_____

_____

_____

_____

_____

BIRDS HARVESTED

Time _____   Gun Used _____

Bullet Weight _____   Number of Pulls _____

Days at Camp _____   Dogs _____

Guide _____   Equipment Used _____

[   ]_____   [   ]_____

[   ]_____   [   ]_____

——— PRIZE PHOTO ———

BIRD HUNTED: _____

> *Will a bird fall into a snare on the earth,*
> *where there is no trap for it? Will a snare spring up*
> *from the earth, if it has caught nothing at all?*
> *Amos 3:5*

Date _____

Location _____

Weather _____

Hunting Partners _____

_____

NOTES

Thoughts and Comments of the Day

_____

_____

_____

_____

_____

_____

_____

_____

_____

Birds Harvested

Time _____   Gun Used _____

Bullet Weight _____   Number of Pulls _____

Days at Camp _____   Dogs _____

Guide _____   Equipment Used _____

[   ]_____   [   ]_____

[   ]_____   [   ]_____

——— PRIZE PHOTO ———

BIRD HUNTED: _____

> *As the deer pants for the water brooks,*
> *So pants my soul for You, O God.*
> *Psalms 42:1b*

Date _____

Location _____

Weather _____

Hunting Partners _____

_____

NOTES

Thoughts and Comments of the Day

_____

_____

_____

_____

_____

_____

_____

_____

_____

BIRDS HARVESTED

Time _____   Gun Used _____

Bullet Weight _____   Number of Pulls _____

Days at Camp _____   Dogs _____

Guide _____   Equipment Used _____

[   ]_____   [   ]_____

[   ]_____   [   ]_____

——— PRIZE PHOTO ———

BIRD HUNTED: _____

> *Your word I have hidden in my heart,*
> *That I might not sin against You!*
> Psalms 119:11

Date _____

Location _____

Weather _____

Hunting Partners _____

_____

NOTES

Thoughts and Comments of the Day

_____

_____

_____

_____

_____

_____

_____

_____

BIRDS HARVESTED

Time _____   Gun Used _____

Bullet Weight _____   Number of Pulls _____

Days at Camp _____   Dogs _____

Guide _____   Equipment Used _____

[   ] _____   [   ] _____

[   ] _____   [   ] _____

———— PRIZE PHOTO ————

BIRD HUNTED: _____

> *Seek good and not evil, That you may live;*
> *So the Lord God of hosts will be with you, As you have spoken.*
> *Amos 5:14*

Date _____

Location _____

Weather _____

Hunting Partners _____

_____

NOTES

Thoughts and Comments of the Day

_____

_____

_____

_____

_____

_____

_____

_____

_____

BIRDS HARVESTED

Time _____   Gun Used _____

Bullet Weight _____   Number of Pulls _____

Days at Camp _____   Dogs _____

Guide _____   Equipment Used _____

[   ]_____   [   ]_____

[   ]_____   [   ]_____

——— PRIZE PHOTO ———

FISHING JOURNAL

Typical Freshwater Fish:

Bass, Largemouth
Bass, Smallmouth
Bass, Striped
Bass, Whiterock
Bluegill
Bowfin
Bream
Buffalo
Bullhead
Burbot
Carp
Catfish
Crappie

Drum
Gar
Grayling
Kokanee
Muskellunge
Oscar
Peacock
Perch
Pickerel
Pike
Redhorse
Roach
Salmon

Sauger
Sturgeon
Sunfish
Tench
Tigerfish
Tilapia
Trout, Brook
Trout, Brown
Trout, Cutthroat
Trout, Lake
Trout, Rainbow
Walleye
Whitefish

Typical Saltwater Fish:

Amberjack
Barracuda
Bass, Black Sea
Bass, Kelp
(Calico)
Bass, Striped
Bluefish
Bonefish
Bonito
Cobia
Cod
Dolphinfish
Drum
Flounder (Flatfishes)
Groupers

Grunts
Halibut
Jack, Almaco
Jacks
Mackerel
Madai
Marlin
Permit
Pollock
Queenfish
Rockfish
Roosterfish
Runner, Rainbow
Sailfish
Seabass

Shark
Sheepshead
Snapper
Snook
Tarpon
Tautog
Trevally
Tripletail
Tuna
Wahoo
Weakfish
Whiting
Yellowtail

FISH: _____ *Largemouth Bass*

> And Jesus, walking by the Sea of Galilee,
> saw two brothers, Simon called Peter, and Andrew his brother,
> casting a net into the sea; for they were fishermen.
> Matthew 4:18

Date _July 15, 2004_

Location _Center Hill Lake, TN_

Weather _Overcast and Hot_

Fishing Partner _John Smith_

and Reggie Johnson

NOTES

Thoughts and Comments of the Day

John, Reggie, and I set off about 5 p.m. We went off to the west to our usual lucky spot in John's new boat. We spent about four hours out on the lake before we called it a day. Just as I was reeling in one last time I hooked a whopper! What a fight!

Fish Caught

Time _8:35 p.m._ Number Caught _14_

Weight _9.2 lbs._ Best of Day _Large mouth_

Length _15.5"_ Fly Used _____

Type _Rod/Reel_ Equipment Used _orange and_

[   ]_____ _Blue spinner_

[   ]_____ _____

—— PRIZE PHOTO ——

Insert Photo of
Largemouth Bass

FISH: _____

> *Simon Peter said to them, "I am going fishing."*
> *They said to him, "We are going with you also."*
> *They went out and immediately got into the boat,*
> *and that night they caught nothing.*
> *John 21:3*

Date _____

Location _____

Weather _____

Fishing Partner _____

_____

NOTES

Thoughts and Comments of the Day

_____
_____
_____
_____
_____
_____
_____
_____
_____

FISH CAUGHT

Time _____   Number Caught _____

Weight _____   Best of Day _____

Length _____   Fly Used _____

Type _____   Equipment Used _____

[   ] _____   _____

[   ] _____   _____

———— PRIZE PHOTO ————

FISH: _____

> *Then He got into one of the boats, which was Simon's,*
> *and asked him to put out a little from the land.*
> *And He sat down and taught the multitudes from the boat.*
> *Luke 5:3*

Date _____

Location _____

Weather _____

Fishing Partner _____

_____

NOTES

Thoughts and Comments of the Day

_____

_____

_____

_____

_____

_____

_____

_____

_____

Fish Caught

Time _____   Number Caught _____

Weight _____   Best of Day _____

Length _____   Fly Used _____

Type _____   Equipment Used _____

[   ]_____   _____

[   ]_____   _____

——— PRIZE PHOTO ———

FISH: _____

> *Be still, and know that I am God;*
> *I will be exalted among the nations,*
> *I will be exalted in the earth!*
> *Psalms 46:10*

Date _____

Location _____

Weather _____

Fishing Partner _____

_____

Thoughts and Comments of the Day

NOTES

_____

_____

_____

_____

_____

_____

_____

_____

Fish Caught

Time _____ Number Caught _____

Weight _____ Best of Day _____

Length _____ Fly Used _____

Type _____ Equipment Used _____

[   ] _____   _____

[   ] _____   _____

——— PRIZE PHOTO ———

FISH: _____

> *And He said to them, "Cast the net on the right side of the boat, and you will find some." So they cast, and now they were not able to draw it in because of the multitude of fish.*
> *John 21:6*

Date _____

Location _____

Weather _____

Fishing Partner _____

_____

NOTES

Thoughts and Comments of the Day

_____
_____
_____
_____
_____
_____
_____
_____
_____

Fish Caught

Time _____   Number Caught _____

Weight _____   Best of Day _____

Length _____   Fly Used _____

Type _____   Equipment Used _____

[   ] _____   _____

[   ] _____   _____

——— PRIZE PHOTO ———

FISH: _____

Jesus said to them,
"Bring some of the fish which you have just caught."
John 21:10

Date _____

Location _____

Weather _____

Fishing Partner _____

_____

NOTES

Thoughts and Comments of the Day

_____
_____
_____
_____
_____
_____
_____
_____
_____

Fish Caught

Time _____   Number Caught _____

Weight _____   Best of Day _____

Length _____   Fly Used _____

Type _____   Equipment Used _____

[   ]_____   _____

[   ]_____   _____

——— PRIZE PHOTO ———

FISH: _____

> *For this is God, Our God forever and ever;*
> *He will be our guide Even to death.*
> *Psalms 48:14*

Date _____

Location _____

Weather _____

Fishing Partner _____

_____

| NOTES |
| |

Thoughts and Comments of the Day

_____
_____
_____
_____
_____
_____
_____
_____
_____

Fish Caught

Time _____   Number Caught _____

Weight _____   Best of Day _____

Length _____   Fly Used _____

Type _____   Equipment Used _____

[   ] _____   _____

[   ] _____   _____

——— PRIZE PHOTO ———

FISH: _____

> *If a son asks for bread from any father among you,*
> *will he give him a stone? Or if he asks for a fish,*
> *will he give him a serpent instead of a fish?*
> *Luke 11:11*

Date _____

Location _____

Weather _____

Fishing Partner _____

_____

NOTES

Thoughts and Comments of the Day

_____

_____

_____

_____

_____

_____

_____

_____

FISH CAUGHT

Time _____   Number Caught _____

Weight _____   Best of Day _____

Length _____   Fly Used _____

Type _____   Equipment Used _____

[   ]_____   _____

[   ]_____   _____

———— PRIZE PHOTO ————

FISH: _____

> But Simon answered and said to Him,
> "Master, we have toiled all night and caught nothing;
> nevertheless at Your word I will let down the net."
> Luke 5:5

Date _____

Location _____

Weather _____

Fishing Partner _____

_____

NOTES

Thoughts and Comments of the Day

_____

_____

_____

_____

_____

_____

_____

_____

_____

Fish Caught

Time _____   Number Caught _____

Weight _____   Best of Day _____

Length _____   Fly Used _____

Type _____   Equipment Used_____

[   ]_____   _____

[   ]_____   _____

———— PRIZE PHOTO ————

FISH: _____

> *Simon Peter went up and dragged the net to land,*
> *full of large fish, one hundred and fifty-three;*
> *and although there were so many, the net was not broken.*
> *John 21:11*

Date _____

Location _____

Weather _____

Fishing Partner _____

_____

NOTES

Thoughts and Comments of the Day

_____
_____
_____
_____
_____
_____
_____
_____
_____

Fish Caught

Time _____   Number Caught _____

Weight _____   Best of Day _____

Length _____   Fly Used _____

Type _____   Equipment Used _____

[   ] _____   _____

[   ] _____   _____

——— PRIZE PHOTO ———

FISH: _____

> *When He had stopped speaking, He said to Simon,*
> *"Launch out into the deep and let down your nets for a catch."*
> *Luke 5:4*

Date _____

Location _____

Weather _____

Fishing Partner _____

_____

NOTES

Thoughts and Comments of the Day

_____

_____

_____

_____

_____

_____

_____

_____

_____

_____

FISH CAUGHT

Time _____   Number Caught _____

Weight _____   Best of Day _____

Length _____   Fly Used _____

Type _____   Equipment Used _____

[   ]_____   _____

[   ]_____   _____

———— PRIZE PHOTO ————

FISH: _____

> *Therefore do not worry about tomorrow,*
> *for tomorrow will worry about its own things.*
> *Sufficient for the day is its own trouble.*
> Matthew 6:34

Date _____

Location _____

Weather _____

Fishing Partner _____

_____

NOTES

Thoughts and Comments of the Day

_____
_____
_____
_____
_____
_____
_____
_____
_____

FISH CAUGHT

Time _____   Number Caught _____

Weight _____   Best of Day _____

Length _____   Fly Used _____

Type _____   Equipment Used _____

[   ] _____   _____

[   ] _____   _____

———— PRIZE PHOTO ————

FISH: _____

> *Then He said to them, "Follow Me,*
> *and I will make you fishers of men."*
> *They immediately left their nets and followed Him.*
> *Matthew 4:19, 20*

Date _____

Location _____

Weather _____

Fishing Partner _____

_____

NOTES

Thoughts and Comments of the Day

_____

_____

_____

_____

_____

_____

_____

_____

_____

FISH CAUGHT

Time _____ Number Caught _____

Weight _____ Best of Day _____

Length _____ Fly Used _____

Type _____ Equipment Used _____

[   ]_____   _____

[   ]_____   _____

————— PRIZE PHOTO —————

FISH: _____

> *And Jesus said to Simon, "Do not be afraid.*
> *From now on you will catch men." So when they had*
> *brought their boats to land, they forsook all and followed Him.*
> *Luke 5:10*

Date _____

Location _____

Weather _____

Fishing Partner _____

_____

Thoughts and Comments of the Day

NOTES

_____

_____

_____

_____

_____

_____

_____

_____

FISH CAUGHT

Time _____   Number Caught _____

Weight _____   Best of Day _____

Length _____   Fly Used _____

Type _____   Equipment Used _____

[   ] _____   _____

[   ] _____   _____

——— PRIZE PHOTO ———

Thoughts & Reflections

_____

_____

_____

_____

_____

_____

_____

_____

_____

_____

_____

_____

_____

_____

_____

_____

_____

_____

Thoughts & Reflections

_____

_____

_____

_____

_____

_____

_____

_____

_____

_____

_____

_____

_____

_____

_____

_____

_____

_____

_____

Thoughts & Reflections

THOUGHTS & REFLECTIONS

_____

_____

_____

_____

_____

_____

_____

_____

_____

_____

_____

_____

_____

_____

_____

_____

_____

_____

_____

Thoughts & Reflections

_____

_____

_____

_____

_____

_____

_____

_____

_____

_____

_____

_____

_____

_____

_____

_____

_____

_____

_____